ON CHRISTIAN RULERS

Sedulius Scotus

Translated by: D.P. Curtin

Dalcassian Publishing Company
PHILADELPHIA, PA

Copyright @ 2010 Dalcassian Publishing Company

All rights reserved. No part of this publication may be reproduced, distributed, or transmitted in any form or by any means, including photocopying, recording, or other electronic or mechanical methods, without the prior written permission of the publisher, except in the case of brief quotations embodied in critical reviews and certain other non-commercial uses permitted by copyright law. For permission request, write to Dalcassian Publishing Company at dalcassianpublishing at gmail.com

ISBN: 979-8-8690-9445-2 (Paperback)

Library of Congress Control Number:
Author: Curtin, D.P. (1985-)

Printed by Ingram Content Group, 1 Ingram Blvd, La Vergne, Tennessee

First printing edition 2010.

ON CHRISTIAN RULERS

THE PREFACE OF THE NEXT WORK BEGINNING.

Every trifid service that presides in the world,
to be governed by art. There are many gifts of art.
The omnicreating Lord creates
the earth, the sea, the stars, and the heavens by art, and rules the whole
beautiful world by art.
By excellent arts, the lofty wisdom of the Thunderer
placed man above all the animals of the world.
Art directs the chariot, art directs the ships properly,
And a triumphant thing looks to the art of war.
He needs craft bees. So that the state may be happy,

with a good ruler and a happy people.
On account of this heavenly passage across the meadows of
Florida books, I have collected for you, king, the illustrious sheaves,
Which will crown your head with the diadem of your mind,
And glorify the scepter of Christ's dominion with a nod,
And the salutary herbs of the divine dogma
I have plucked with my thumb in baskets smelling of nard.
Take the waves from Israel's liquid fountains
Which will satisfy the drink of the pre-sweet dew.
For the glory of kings, their shining scepters, and their scepters,
are the Dogmas of the Lord, and not only the examples of the former,
and the exploits of noble nobles, famous throughout the world.
By these arts may your victorious state prosper,
And may it be ruled happily for many years,
Until you ascend the starry hall,
The just reigning with which eternal glory will rule.
The preface is explicit.
With you is the beginning, the end, the king and Christ, with you.
Be the servant of the Alpha work, God, and yours.

THE CHAPTERS OF THAT BOOK BEGINS.

I. *Concerning the fact that a pious ruler, having received royal power, must first pay dignified honors to God and the holy churches.*
II. *How should an orthodox king govern himself?*
III. *By this skill and energy a momentary kingdom may be established*
IV. *Kingly power is not so much to be adorned with riches and confidence of strength, as with wisdom and the worship of piety.*
V. *How much sacred care and concern must be shown by him towards his wife and children and his own household.*
VI. *The kind of counselors and friends a good leader should have.*
VII. *These things make bad leaders.*
VIII. *Of greedy or impious kings, and how many evils are caused by the same people, or divine vengeance follows them.*
IX. *Of the peaceful and merciful king. Or to whom benefits should be given.*
X. *How many pillars support the kingdom of a just king?*
XI. *On the fact that a good leader should favor ecclesiastical causes with benevolent and earnest concern and synodal meetings.*
XII. *On the fact that it is glorious to obey a pious ruler with the most salutary admonitions and reproofs of his predecessor.*
XIII *Of the zeal of a good ruler mixed with reason and piety.*
XIV. *About the Christian leader, so that he does not trust in his own strength and that of his people, but in the Lord.*
XV. *Concerning the fact that in the impending destruction of hostile wars, divine help is to be implored.*
XVI. *Of the adversities that may happen.*
XVII. *Of not being proud after peace has been offered even by the enemy, or enemies have been prostrated.*
XVIII. *Thanks and benevolent wishes to be returned to God after peace or victory.*
XIX. *Of the privileges of the holy mother Church to be preserved by the pious governor, and of the dignified superiors and ministers of the churches.*
XX. *How many disgraces the proud, and what kind or how much glory accompanies the orthodox princes here and in the future.*

THE BOOK OF SEDULUS BEGINNING ABOUT THE CHRISTIAN PRINCIPLES AND CONVENIENT RULES BY WHICH PUBLIC AFFAIRS ARE TO BE GOVERNED RIGHTEOUSLY.

CHAPTER ONE. After the Christian governor has taken up the royal scepter and the helms of the kingdom, he must first render thanksgivings and worthy honors to the Almighty and to the holy Church. Indeed, the public affairs are then most beautifully consecrated in their beginning, when royal solicitude and sacred devotion to the saint of the heavenly king are kindled at the same time by fear and love; since the glorious benefit of the Church is procured by a providential counsel; that whom the royal purple and the other insignia of the kingdom adorn outwardly, the same praiseworthy vows towards God and the holy Church inwardly pervade him; because, of course, the summit of the temporal kingdom is then markedly ascended, when the glory or honor of the omnipotent king is pursued with pious zeal. Pius, therefore, the prince of the supreme donor, should strive very hard to obey the will and holy precepts of all, by whose heavenly will and ordinance he has no doubt that he has ascended to the summit of the government, testifying to the Apostle who says: There is no power except from God; but those things which are, were ordained by God (Rom. 13:1). In so far as a good ruler knows that he has been ordained by God, he watches over with pious care, so far as he arranges and weighs everything in an orderly manner before God and men according to the balance of righteousness. For what are the Christian leaders of the people, but ministers of the Almighty? Moreover, everyone is a worthy and faithful minister, if he does with sincere devotion what his master and teacher has commanded him. Hence the most pious and glorious princes rejoice to be called and to be ministers and servants of the Most High rather than lords or kings of men. Hence the blessed king David, and the great prophet, often calls himself the servant of the Lord. And not even the famous Solomon, the same son, supplicating the Almighty, says among other things: Look at the prayer of your servant and at his prayers, Lord my God; listen to the hymn and the prayer that your servant is praying before you today, so that your eyes may be opened on the house of which you said: My name will be there (3 Kings 8, 28, 29).

Hence also the great emperor Constantine of the most famous memory, believing and perfecting the saving mystery of the cross and the Catholic faith, when his reign was rejoicing, religion also flourished greatly, not being arrogant to himself, but giving thanks to Almighty God, because the God of his plan had deigned to have him as a suitable minister. Behold, the most eminent emperor congratulated himself more that he was the servant of God than that he had an earthly empire. From this he himself, because he had been the minister of the divine will, extended a peaceful kingdom from the British sea to the places of the East; and since he had submitted himself to the Almighty, he powerfully and faithfully overcame all the hostile wars that were waged under him. He was building and endowing the churches with the abundant resources of Christ. Hence the grace of heaven granted him triumphant victories. Because there is no doubt that the more the sacred governors humbly submit themselves to the King of kings, the more they rise sublimely to the eminence of glorious dignity. But who does not wonder how many honors the aforesaid Solomon paid to the Lord, after he had received the scepter of the kingdom by God? With what wise devotion did he build the temple of the Lord and wonderfully decorate it? How many peaceable sacrifices did he offer to God? From this he perceived the fruit of his devotion and prayer, as the Lord appeared to him and spoke, saying: I heard your prayer and the supplication which you pleaded before me; I have sanctified this house which you have built, that I may place my name there forever; and my eyes and my heart shall be there all the days. If you also walk before me, as your father walked in simplicity of heart and in equity, and do all that I have commanded you, and keep my laws and my judgments, I will set the throne of your kingdom over Israel forever, as I spoke to David your father, saying : A man from the throne of Israel shall not be taken from your family (3 Kings 9, 3-5). Therefore, if that king Solomon, for his sacred devotion and for building the earthly house of the Lord, earned so much glory of reward, how inestimable will he have the palm of glory if a ruler beloved of God adorns the holy Church, which is the spiritual tabernacle of the living God? But these things which we have said briefly in the style of prose, let us conclude with some sweet verses.

Whoever carries the flourishing scepter of the noble kingdom,
let him offer his wishes and prayers to the First Celsitron.
In whose sanctuary are all the scepters of the god,
and the peace of the nobles, the life and safety of the leaders.
For the royal glory and crown of the kingdom
is the fear of the high throne and the holy love of God.
The lilies of the field, or the milky
field, as the rose blushes with the pink outline,
So the just ruler of the virtues grows green,
Germinates like the sacred fruits of the mind in the citadel.
The fair purple adorned Solomon the king,
Nor David's bright scepter of his father,
But more inwardly the prudent devotion of the heart
Decorated the young man glorifying God.
Let your state shine like a lucifer,
And bring bright wishes in the new spring.

CHAPTER II. He who ascends to the pinnacle of royal dignity, superior to the Lord, must first rule himself, whom the divine disposition has ordained to rule others. For a king is called by ruling. Then let him understand that he is truly called by this name, who does not know how to govern himself rationally. An orthodox king, therefore, should endeavor supremely, so that he who desires to rule well over his subjects, and arranges to correct the errors of others, himself does not admit evils, which the evil one strictly corrects, and strives before all to fulfill the good things he commands. Now in six ways a good governor governs himself commendably: first, while he represses illicit thoughts with severity of mind; secondly, while he is discussing salutary policies pertaining both to his own interest and to that of the people; thirdly, when idle and useless or noxious leaves of empty words avoid flowing forth; fourthly, when the prudence of glorious princes will at the same time sweeten the words, and also the words of the divine Scriptures, upon the honey and honeycomb of the mind's palate; fifthly, when perpetrating every dishonor of a destructive action, he is afraid; But in the sixth place, if they are laudable, if they are of a glorious disposition, he should show in a remarkable manner the magnificent works, so that he who inwardly shines before the Lord with a devout will, may outwardly shine before the people in word and deed. It is proper to observe the three rules, that is, terror, order, and love. For unless he is loved and feared at the same time, his organization cannot be established at all. Therefore, by affability and favors, he should seek to be loved, and by just revenge, he should strive not for his own victory, but for the law of God, so that he may be feared. He must therefore be humble in his own eyes, as it is written: They have made you a leader, do not exalt yourself, but be among them as one of them (Ecclesiastes 32:1). And not only just to men, but to be dominated by the passions of one's body and soul, inasmuch as one may rightly be called a ruler, as a wise man says: He will be a king who will do right; he who will not do, will not be. Therefore let him be most prudent in his speech, now that he may be terrible; but more often the grace of sweetness affable, the conqueror of lust, pride, and vexing ferocity, the friend of the good and the enemy of tyrants, the enemy of crimes, the enemy of vices, the most cautious in war, the most steadfast in peace, the most approved by faithful promises, putting the divine before the human, deterring his subjects from evil, inviting them to good, rewarding abundance, liberating indulgence, making good out of evil, making the best out of good. Let him be holy and useful to the state, commendable in his clemency, conspicuous in his goodness, excellent in piety, fortitude, chastity, and justice, the best man and most worthy of the crown of the prince, always having the fear of God before his eyes, and according to the decrees of the Almighty, weighing just judgments, who gives salvation to kings, and he does all that he wills in heaven and on earth and in every creature; because he is the Lord of all, to whom every knee bows of the heavenly, earthly, and infernal (Phil. 2:10), in whose hand is all power in heaven and on earth, who is the king of kings, and the hope of glory of just and righteous rulers.

> *He who governs the affections of the soul is rightly called a king,*
> *and he who tames the temptations of the flesh.*
> *Although he who surpasses the yellow in prowess,*
> *let the King hold a clear place of honor and praise;*
> *But it is more praiseworthy to trample*
> *on the pride of the proud;*
> *He is great, and he hears the savages who crush the enemy,*
> *Lauriger and the victor bring back bright trophies.*
> *Glory, but a greater reckoning, that with heavenly weapons*
> *I should be able to vanquish the airy foes.*

There is more power to restrain the mind by art,
than if a man had three times the wealth of the world.
For the temple of the Lord shines with the royal mind of the righteous,
God himself becomes the throne of the high judgment.
That yellow house is more beautiful than gold, and
the sun of justice is glad to have its own.

CHAPTER III. The momentary kingdom of this age is judged by the wise to be like the whirling wheels of the vertigo. For just as every turning of a wheel casts down that which is superior to it and lifts up that which has been cast down to a higher one, so the earthly glory of the kingdom sustains sudden erections, sudden elisions; whence he has honors which are not true, but imaginary and rather fugitive. For that is the true kingdom, which lasts forever; but this, which is transitory and fleeting, does not show the truth, but a certain moderate likeness of the true and ever-permanent kingdom. For just as the bow of the sky, painted with various colors, quickly retreats with its arched curve, so surely the dignity of worldly glory, although adorned for the present, is still more quickly fleeting. With what skill, and with what energy, and with what concern, is this instability restrained to some semblance of stability? Is it possible that the earthly kingdom is established either by the violent force of arms, or by the peaceful concord of tranquility? But again, it is seen that there is great instability in the weapons and the crashes of wars. For what is more uncertain and more unstable in the events of war, where there is no certain outcome of a laborious struggle, no certain victory, and oftentimes the superior are overcome by the inferior, but sometimes evils approaching each other equally occur; and those who presumed to have victory, both have in the end nothing but calamitous misery. Who can explain how many evils are brought about under the false name of peace? when even that peace, which was believed to be stable and firm between the good, is sometimes translated into deadly storms of discord by the perverse designs of the wicked. Hence instability in arms seems to pass away in peace.

What else remains, then, but that the king's heart and all the confidence of hope should be fixed, not in the strength of arms and men, nor in the illusions of transitory peace, but in the clemency of the Almighty? who knows how to establish the kingdom which he has given, whether in adversity or in prosperity.

The heart of the prince, therefore, and the devotion of the faithful in the government of the ministry, did not forsake him by whom so much benefit and glorious service was bestowed; lest perhaps that supreme ruler, indignant, withdraw from him the benefit which he had given, if he felt that he was unfaithful whom he had ordained as a faithful minister. For if an earthly king is able to take away the power given to him from any unfaithful man, and give it to others whom he finds to be more faithful, how much more is the heavenly giver of the universe, whom the clouds of treachery cannot deceive, able to withdraw benefits from his reprobates, and bestow them on others whom he knows to be worthy ministers of his will. to be? Wherefore even that impious Saul, king of Israel, was deprived of his kingdom and life, because he was not a faithful minister before the Lord. But indeed, David found a man chosen after his own heart by the Almighty, whom he exalted to the pinnacle of royal power, because he had chosen him as a faithful minister in advance. Therefore, a wise ruler should try to establish his heart in the grace of the Most High, if he wishes the transitory kingdom entrusted to him to have some semblance of stability. And since the Lord is just and merciful, to whom he must cleave with the affection of the heart, let him show many works of mercy, that he may reap the glory of a great reward. Let him love justice and at the same time keep it; indeed, he repudiates unjust and malicious deeds in his subjects, and corrects them with praiseworthy zeal, which is according to knowledge. As long as he is stable in the divine precepts, his kingdom is established more and more in this world, and he is led to the joys of eternal stability by heavenly help.

As the cycle of the wheel
Rolls with rapid recursion and represses the highest to the lowest
Which parts it rotates swiftly along the axis
With motion:
Thus the world's trifid reigns Through the orb
of Glory they do not know how to stabilize the lofty summit,
But they know how to fall but have
Golden scepters.
The glory of the Floridian kingdom
of Israel was lifted up by the inglorious people,
when they observed the sacrosanct laws of
the Mystic Law.

Wherefore he was proud of the Lord's triumphs,
And overcame cruel foes,
While he glorified the thundering piety of his people.
Again, alas! How much he is pressed by the ruins
of Abraham, the special saint of his father,
While he was prone to his creator
to submit his neck!
One but the medicine of such a nation
has already been with the hope of begging the heavenly One,
who knows how to establish kingdoms
with a perpetual nod.
Bring the princes of the earth to the mighty Lord,
rejoicing in the blessed incense,
Whom the nobles of heaven tremble with
the Magnificat.

CHAPTER IV. But all royal power, which is divinely established for the benefit of the state, is not so much to be adorned with ephemeral works and earthly strength, as with wisdom and divine worship; since there is no doubt then that the people will be governed by the skill of the provident counsel, the adversaries will be spared by the propitiation of the Lord, and the provinces and the kingdom will be preserved, if the kingdom is exalted by religion and wisdom. For God willed the nature of man to be this, that man himself should be fond of and desirous of two things, religion and wisdom. But religious wisdom is a salutary adornment, a light for the souls of the devout, a heavenly gift and joy that will last without end. He, therefore, who wishes to rule gloriously, and to govern the people wisely, and to be vigorous in his counsels, must ask for wisdom from the Lord, who gives to all abundantly, and does not reproach (James 1:5), and he must seek that wisdom diligently, with labor at the same time and with love. In as much as it corresponds to what is written: Blessed is he who finds wisdom, and he who abounds in prudence (Prov. 3:13), and the rest that are described in the praises of wisdom. That ruler, therefore, is truly blessed to be celebrated, who is illuminated by the splendor of wisdom, which is the source of counsels, the source of sacred religion, the crown of princes, the origin of virtues, in comparison of which all the brilliancy of precious gems pales in comparison. She is very careful in her plans, wonderful in her speeches, magnificent in her works, strong in adversity, temperate in her successes, clear-eyed in her judgments. This grace beautifies her lovers from heaven, and glorifies them like a starry firmament, as it is written: The righteous shall shine like the stars, and the intelligent like the firmament.

This exalted Solomon above all the kings of the earth, because he loved her from his youth, and he became a lover of her beauty. Hence, as it is read in the books of Kings, the Lord appeared to Solomon in a dream at night, saying: Ask what you want, and I will give it to you (4 Kings 2:9). When Solomon, when he was a child, demanded a teachable heart, that he might judge the Lord's people, and distinguish between good and evil, he received such an answer from the Lord: Because thou hast demanded this word, and hast not asked for thyself many days, nor riches, nor the souls of thine enemies, but You asked for wisdom to discern judgment, behold, I have done for you according to your words, and I have given you a wise and understanding heart to such an extent that no one before you was like you, and no one will arise after you. But I also gave you these things which you did not ask for, namely, riches and glory, so that there was no one like you among the kings in all the past days. But if you walk in my ways, and keep my precepts and my commandments, as your father David walked, I will make your days long (3 Kings 3, 11-14). O how ineffable is the bounty of divine grace! which, if asked with the right heart and a pious intention, gives more than what is asked. Behold, King Solomon did not ask for silver, or gold, or other earthly riches, but the gifts of wisdom from the Lord. But he who had rightly asked for the simple, received double. For he was not only enriched by wisdom, but also exalted by the glory of the kingdom. Wherefore an excellent example is given to the kings of the earth, in so far as they desire spiritual gifts more than carnal ones by a pious desire from the Almighty, if they desire to reign long and happily in this world. Therefore, it is fitting that a prince who is lovable to God should have the will and desires of heavenly things. For in this way he truly has his heart in the hand of God, and he will rule the kingdom with peace for many years, with the favor of the Lord.

> *He who wishes to be a righteous ruler and judge,*
> *Lance who rejoices in the just and balanced,*
> *Inhians to drill the lies of the beautiful*
> *on the cusp of truth,*

He who creates the
bright father of the Sun and the moon, and the shining cosmos,
bids the senses shine with the twinkling
light of Sophia.
May Solomon's fair ones know
what they flew suddenly through the ether,
and penetrated
the golden roofs of the Lord's sabbath.
He himself perceived the docile sense
of the mind and became wise.
In addition, the pillar of the kingdom governs
the Jewish nation.
What is the value of all the yellow glitter of gold?
What good are oysters for the beauty of the rose?
What are the Scythian glories and jewels?
What is the diadem?
If the orb dims the edge of the mind,
the light cannot protect the truth,
so that it can distinguish good, bad, just, and good
and bad.
Therefore, it is fitting for a ruler to love
You, the Word of the Father and the wise light,
O Christ, who rules the world with a scepter
and reigns supreme.
On whose right hand rests the blessed
Constance, and on the left the rich and rich gauze.
The prince of glory crowning the lowly
Tollis the rich.

CHAPTER V. A pious and wise king carries out the service of governing in three ways. For the first is himself, as we have shown in the foregoing; secondly, his own wife and his children and household; thirdly, he must govern the people entrusted to him with rational and glorious control. A good prince, therefore, must not only rule himself, so long as he declines from evils, and chooses and holds firmly to what is good; but he also governs others who join him, that is, his wife, children, and household, with provident care and familial charity. And by doing this, he treasures up for himself a double palm of glory, so that while he is good and holy in himself, he makes others conjoined to him good and holy, according to the Psalmist, who says: With a holy man you will be holy, and with an innocent man you will be innocent (Ps. 17:27), and the rest. For it is not enough to have one's own honesty, unless one is chaste and chaste with one's spouse, nor is one also adorned with the modesty of one's children and companions and servants, as David said: He walked in an undefiled way, he ministered to me (Ps. 00:6). For as the lily of the field is beautified by the manifold beauty of other flowers and violets, and as the moon shines more favorably with the brightness of the stars around it, so surely a just and wise king will be born in the company of other good people. Therefore he should see to it that he has not only a noble, beautiful and rich man, but also a chaste, prudent one, and one steeped in holy virtues. For in proportion as the conjugation is a conjunction in law, so much is it either harmful by the ferocity of malice, or sweet by the sweetness of manners. Indeed, a foolish woman is the ruin of a house, the failure of riches, the satiety of the wicked, the abode of all evils and vices; which adorns itself outwardly with various superstitions, but does not know how to adorn the interior of its soul. Whom he loves today, he hates tomorrow. And as someone says: A woman unfaithful to her husband is a shipwreck. Thus, on the other hand, a chaste and prudent woman, disciplined intent on useful things, governs her children and family peacefully with a low face and cheerful speech, and for the sake of her husband's safety, if necessary, she opposes her life to death, and guards the riches that are her husbands with a good reputation. He who was his friend yesterday is his friend today. There is therefore the very bringing forth of riches, and the strengthening of the house, the delight of the husband, the beauty of the family, and the connection of all the virtues. And such a one ought not only to be a chaste couple attached to and submissive to her husband, but always to show a form of piety and holy conduct, and to be a rehearser of prudent counsel. For as by the persuasion of an evil spouse harmful dangers are born, so by the counsel of a prudent wife many useful things result, which are well-pleasing to the Almighty. Hence the Apostle also says that an unbelieving man will be saved through a faithful woman (1 Cor. 7:14).

And not only unbelievers, but also holy and orthodox princes, often weigh and listen to prudence in their wives, not considering the fragile sex, but reaping the fruits of good counsel. Hence it is also related to the venerable wife of the glorious emperor Theodosius, named Placilla, that the prince himself, while he was in himself good and just and wise, had also another opportunity of advantage by which he would triumph over good works. For his spouse frequently reminded him of the divine laws, while she herself was perfectly educated first. For it was not raised to the heights of the kingdom, but rather inflamed by divine love. For the greatness of the beneficence made the desire of the benefactor greater for him. For suddenly he came to the purple. He took the greatest care of the crippled and the infirm, not using servants, not using other ministers, but acting by himself, and coming to their dwellings, and providing each with what he needed. Even so, running through the xenodochia of the churches, he ministered with his hands to the sick, wiping their pots, tasting the soup, offering spoons, breaking bread and serving food, washing the cup, and doing all the other things that it is customary for servants and ministers to do solemnly. But to those who were endeavoring to prevent such things, he said: To distribute gold is the work of the government; and I offer this work on behalf of the government itself, having given me all good things. For she often said to her husband: It is necessary for you always, husband, to think about what you were a while ago, what you are now. If you always think of these things, you will not be ungrateful to your benefactor, but you will lawfully govern the government which you have undertaken, and you will appease the author of these things. By these words, therefore, he seemed to offer his spouse a certain advantage and an abundance of virtue.

> *A pious and wise king governs himself*
> *and his subjects by the rule of three.*
> *The glory of the ruler's character is proved by his wife,*
> *like an honest vineyard.*
> *That nobility was charmed by the threefold power*
> *of a modest breast.*
> *If the necks are adorned, let them shine with a beautiful milk,*
> *Chastity shines more.*
> *As Christ united the Church to himself in chaste love,*
> *so let the wife cleave to her husband.*
> *Gentle simplicity in whose mind overflows*
> *Like the grace of a dove.*

How beautiful piety, prudence, and sacred power,
Esther flourished like an alma.
The king and the queen
love the bonds of peace.
Envy did not separate the twins by discord of peace
Whom the law above had united.
Discipline governs whose noble branch
may blossom in beauty.
A good cultivator provides that the palm tree may grow green and dry.
If the prince and ruler rule the people properly,
they rule over their descendants.
As Abraham's noble race created,
they adorn the poles of their grandchildren.

CHAPTER VI. In human affairs, as they say, there is no art more difficult than to rule well in the midst of the most turbulent storms of this age, and to govern the state prudently. But this art then reaches the end of perfection, when the state itself has wise and excellent counselors. Now there is a third rule to be observed in counsels; the first, indeed, that the divine should be preferred to the human, since it is necessary to obey God rather than men (Acts 5:29). If anyone, therefore, arranges and desires successfully to steer the ship of the state like a good pilot, let him not neglect the best counsels of the Lord, which have been set forth in the sacred discourses. But the second rule is that of counsel, inasmuch as a prudent ruler relies not so much on his own counsel as on that of the wisest of his people. Hence this was always the chief opinion of the emperor Antoninus in his counseling: It is fairer that I should follow the advice of so many such friends, than that so many such friends should follow the will of one of mine. Solomon also attests to this very thing, who says: Thoughts are scattered where there is no counsel: but where there are many counselors, they are strengthened (Prov. 15:22), and there will be salvation where there are many counsels (Prov. 11:14). For a wise man calls the wise into counsel and does nothing without their counsel. But a fool thinks within himself, and quickly does what he wills without the advice of others. Moreover, the third principle is to be obtained in counsel, lest a good ruler should have deceitful and destructive ones. For who should trust in the counsels of evildoers? For as valleys in the plains, and snares in the streets, and pegs where they are not supposed, hold back the feet of others, so the plans of the wicked, mingled with fierce wickedness, hinder the just and the holy in their journeys. For good counselors raise up the state, so bad ones precipitate ruinous calamities. Such counselors, then, are to be rejected and detested in every way; because those who despise God's precepts by living badly will never be devoted to an earthly prince. For who can be good, who are bad for themselves?

But just as the most salutary counsels and precepts of Almighty God are to be published, so the counsels of the prudent are sometimes to be concealed from the enemies of the righteous. For in a state there are no better plans than those which the adversary is ignorant of. Indeed, a safe journey is being made, because the enemy does not at all suspect what is to be done. But the two most contrary to counsel are haste and anger. For anger blinds the mind from seeing a good plan, and how long plans generally do not succeed. And then, especially, the plan is carried out to the result of success, when the royal trust is fixed with the help of the Almighty. After God, where do good plans come from, except from faithful and best friends, who hope to be enlightened by divine grace, so that they do not err in their plans? By their providential deliberation, divinely inspiring clemency, the cluster of wholesome counsel is often plucked. It is far from the case that a good prince should have friends who are cruel tyrants, like fierce dragons, because he is modeled after the panther as an animal. For the panther, a kind of quadruped, is, according to scientists, the friend of all animals, except the dragon. Therefore, let him have the friendship of those whom he knows to be righteous. But who are good friends? except those who are holy and venerable, not malicious, not thieves, not partisans, not cunning, not consenting to evil, not enemies of the good, not lustful, not cruel, not besiegers of their prince; but the holy, the restrained, the religious, the lovers of their prince, and those who neither laugh at him themselves, nor wish to be laughed at, who neither lie, nor pretend, and never deceive; but truthful, sober, prudent, and in all things faithful to their prince. With such people, therefore, the state is made safe, and the fame and glory of the pious ruler increases.

> *Away from the rudder the ship sways in the high*
> *waves, and she is battered by the swells,*
> *the glory of the kingdom and*
> *the splendid scepters fall, alas! without advice*

For there are some whose tongue is made of honey,
but under the asps hides a bitter poison.
Those who persuade all things with words,
whose speech is sly or a pit.
It seems that the state supported their decision
Because of this plan to pick up the sweet cluster
When the sunken rushes, O pitiful one too!
It is already fitting for the high one who holds the government.
The Dorcades are like the watchmen of a mountain seen from the top,
where they quickly flee and note all the dangers,
so the adverse things are
carefully watched by the light of the mind.
As the pearls are licked by noble shells,
As sweet flowing honey is read from the honeycomb,
So also friends should be read from the pure fountain
And it is fitting and profitable to counsel.
A true keeper of friendship is proved without fury,
Who likes all good, dislikes all evil.
There is one who does not really know how to say no or no,
whose heart is in tune with the secret and pious.
Olli's firm faith becomes dearer to life itself,
He does not know how to weave reeds with his mind.
The blare of trumpets does not sway him,
for Anchora remains steadfast in her heart of faith.
Neither gauze, nor weights of gold know how
to deceive such, lest the precious faith should be injured.

CHAPTER VII. But now the order expounds that we should briefly summarize some of the bad princes as well, since we have said of the good some that are useful to scepters, which are necessary for the state. In the first place it is asked what causes bad rulers even out of good ones? To which we must reply: First, royal permission, then the abundance of things, when the very abundance of things becomes the cause of evils. Moreover, unscrupulous friends, detestable servants, avaricious eunuchs, courtiers, or fools, or detestable, by whom even in that ruler who seemed to be good, forgetfulness of the commandments of God is born. Finally, what cannot be denied, is ignorance of public affairs. Hence four or five gather themselves together and take one plan to deceive the emperor or the king. They say what must be proved. The emperor who is shut up at home does not know the truth; he is compelled only by what they speak; Hence also a good and prudent and excellent commander is sold, who is made miserable by that very fact when truths are withheld from him. For this reason, piety and truth are often oppressed by tumultuous indiscipline and God's knife, when much derogation prevails when the detractors are believed to be worthy of faith, whom the twin plagues corrupt most bitterly, that is, the love of falsity and the hatred of truth.

How rushing the whirlwind
overthrew the multitude of things!
Those who first shine in the rule of good
often become profane by the end of evil.
Those who were sacred in their morals were gold,
Soon those like lead are cheaply horrified.
And those who were happy to give birth to the vines,
grow like scornful scorn.
The unwary lord, with his mind atrophied,
So too his friends fall.
By many tricks thence the best
Anceps becomes, trembling like a reed,
And ignores the wretched figments of falsehood,
Nor do the lights of truth shine upon the master.
For the king's eyes are blinded by honors,
gold, riches, clouds, lies,
the flattering pleasure of a woman's face,
false charms, pomp, and power.

CHAPTER VIII. It seems to be the only consequence, so far as we have discussed of impious rulers, that recognizing their wickedness and worst in the end of this world, in a perpetual manner, the prudent ruler, by abstaining from evil works, becomes more cautious and better, and greatly seeks to please the supreme benefactor. But what are impious kings, if not the greatest robbers of the world, fierce as lions, mad as bears? as it is written of him: A roaring lion and a hungry bear, a wicked ruler over a poor people (Prov. 28:15). For the wicked king, having the person of a lion, fiercely responds to every answer by uttering an evil word with all malice without the advice of the prudent, humiliating the good and exalting the bad. whose days shall be shortened, and his memory shall perish with the noise. For he sinned more than he could. Such, then, are the friends of the evil, the enemies of the good, the servants of lust and avarice, the servants of all wickedness, the servants of the devil, always laboring and doing nothing, the gurgles of the human race, of misery, fodder for eternal hell, like cedars suddenly exalted, but plunged into the depths of tartar. Hence the Psalmist says: I saw the wicked exalted and exalted like the cedars of Lebanon, and I passed by and behold, he was not, and I sought him, and his place was not found (Ps. 36, 35, 36). For they flourish like the herbs and grass of the field, which to-day spring up with beauty, and to-morrow are not found withered. Of whom it is said through the prophet: They reigned, and not from me; There were princes, and I was ignorant; who neither knew nor wanted to walk in the right and royal way but know how to turn to the right and to the left. To them belongs that which the Lord speaks through Isaiah, saying: They have forsaken the Lord of hosts, and have walked in crooked ways (Isa. 1:4). Deceitful in their plans, cruel and deceitful in their words, malicious in their deeds, whose end will be according to their deeds. Of whom it is said by the same prophet: The Lord of hosts thought to bring down the pride of all glory, and to bring down to shame the disgrace of the earth (Isa. 23:9). But also, the blessed Job: Praise, he says, is a short reign, and the glory of a hypocrite is like a point (Job 20:5). Indeed, this temporal life is compared to the smallest point in comparison with eternity. Woe to those who sell the glory of eternal happiness for a small point of present happiness!

But it is not in our power to tell how much evil will befall either the subjects themselves or the divine vengeance upon the rulers themselves; but I would like to make a few out of many into the manifest. King Pharaoh's impiety, which he had inculcated from the hardness of his heart, brought ten plagues on himself and his Egyptians, and in addition drowned himself and his people in the Red Sea and the Tartars of Acheron. Antiochus and Herod and Pontius Pilate, who does not know with what vengeance the district judge struck? What shall I say of Nero, Aegeus, and the impious Julian, and others like them in wickedness? Did not all of them with their followers after death be devoured by the worst mouth of hell? But to pass over the innumerable, I will explain the unfortunate end of this world of Theodoric, the most cruel king, who, being a jealous follower of Arians, and a persecutor of the good Christians, finally, as it had been revealed to a certain man, was torn between John the pope and Symmachus the patrician, and trampled underfoot, and led away with bound hands, in He threw the pot to Vulcan. For because he had slain John in custody by afflicting the pope, he also slew the patrician Symmachus with a sword, and appeared thrown into the fire by those whom he had unjustly judged in this life. O how severe and just are the judgments of the Almighty! at the disposition of which a nod worthy of vengeance followed the tyrant mercilessly. For he who unjustly inflicted transitory death upon the servants of the Lord, justly perishes by the double death of body and soul. He who had robbed others of this present life, was himself robbed of both momentary and eternal life. And so the twin performed the same service; for to himself the punishment of hell, where he will be tormented forever and ever, but to the saints he administered the palm of heavenly glory. The unjustly judged are suddenly crowned, and the judges have been passed over by the Lord as cruel tyrants. But he who judges unjustly is suddenly judged and given up to the flames of eternal damnation. In this matter a very terrible example is set forth, lest the mighty of the earth should persecute the servants of the Lord, whom the mighty God avenges with the mighty arm of his power. But let these things be said of the reprobates to the rulers. Now let's move on to the more important consequence of the style.

> *Do the kings of the earth, who are disfigured by evil deeds,*
> *seem like*
> *wild boars, bears, and tigers?*
> *Are these greater*
> *Terrigen robbers, rabid lions,*
> *ravenous hawks with claws?*
> *It happened to Antiochus and Pharaoh,*
> *Herod and the miserable Pilate*
> *to lose their kingdoms for a moment, and*
> *to undergo Acheron with their allies.*
> *Thus, the reprobate always*
> *suffer evil losses too here and in the age.*
> *What are the blossoming seasons of the children*

Burning and the beauty of the thorn,
Whom the furnace of fire awaits,
Whom the dewy rain will not hurt?
Those who do not love the Lord of light, will go
into the outer darkness;
there your glory
will wither without end.
But the righteous will be glorified by a lofty crown
and a blessed light.

CHAPTER IX. The seven are more beautiful than the other creatures of God, as the wise say, when the cloudless sky is compared with a wonderful likeness of silver color; the sun in its power, when it illuminates the inhabitants of the world in the brightness of its glory with reciprocal courses; the moon in its integrity and naked face with retreating clouds, when it traces the tracks of the sun in its own course; a fruitful field, when it is depicted with different flowers and curling knots; the variety of the sea, when the serenity of the sky and the placid waves of the clouds are most beautifully displayed on the shores; a chorus of righteous people living in one faith; a peaceful king in the glory of his kingdom, when in the royal court he bestows many favors with presents and gifts handed down. Indeed, a just and peaceful king divides goods with a cheerful countenance, and carefully ponders the cause of each one, and not looking down on the weak and poor of the people, he speaks true judgments with the advice and judgment of the elders and prudent, humiliating the bad and exalting the good. His days will be extended with glory, and his memory will remain forever. The peaceable prince is like a flowery and fertile paradise in the neighborhood, and like an honorable vineyard abounding in copious fruit, disturbing all discord by the splendor of his sight, who, while he embraces peace in the court of his mind, undoubtedly prepares a dwelling place for Christ, because Christ is peace, and in peace he wants to rest. Moreover, where there is peace, truth is found in discussions, and justice in works. As, therefore, a prudent pilot endeavors to escape the dangers of a stormy sea by the smiling serenity of time, so a peaceful ruler, with a serene calmness of mind, and the harmony of peace, plans to check the attacks of discord by diligent deliberation. Which three rules of peace must be preserved, namely: above oneself, in oneself, next to oneself; because he must be peaceful towards God, both within himself and around his neighbors. For the good of peace is so great, that even in earthly and mortal things, nothing is more pleasing to be heard, nothing more desirable to be desired, nothing better finally to be found. But the fruit of a peaceful mind is to show kindness to subjects and friends, at the same time mercy and clemency, by which virtues both a pious ruler and his kingdom are gloriously preserved; witnessing Solomon, who said: Mercy and truth guard the king, and clemency will strengthen his throne (Prov. 20, 28). For there is nothing that better recommends a good ruler, favorable and lovable to the people, than clemency and peaceful serenity.

These things, that I may omit the others for the sake of brevity, made Augustus Caesar the most famous; this he exalted Antoninus, also the great Constantine, Theodosius, and the rest of the great princes. He also dedicated the same great Charles, among other insignia of virtue, to Augustus, the most sacred of all princes of the world. This appointed Louis the most pious emperor. And what more shall I say? Surely the most serene mercy of mercy has glorified glorious princes on earth and placed the consorts of the saints in heaven. Who gave not only their own, but also their whole selves to the Almighty. But nothing is to be given by a just and pious king, unless it is a boon. But the benefit, if it is related to some kind of remuneration in this world, is destroyed and finished. For we cannot have it whole, the price of which has been paid to us. Wherefore such a bounty should be called not so much a benefit, but rather a trade. Indeed, benefits which do not harm the reputation, piety, and justice of a good prince should be given according to the dignity of persons and the interests of things, not according to the desires of those who receive them, who easily deny themselves; because that which is difficult or impossible, they expound impiously and atrociously. Hence the emperor Nerva said: When friends presume to deserve everything, if they have not extorted anything, they become more terrible. Therefore, in all temporal gifts a measure must be observed, and a right intention in giving, so that for the safety of the state and the holy benefit of the Church, and for the sake of the heavenly indignities of glory, all things are distributed to the best and the best, through the generosity of the serene prince.

The creator of the heavenly world, the ruler of all things,
He himself, the artist, made everything that he created beautiful.

Among these creations, seven preeminent ones stand out,
Painted by the sphere of heaven with the shining grace of light,
Soul of the sun among the stars and shining glory,
And full behind the two-horned moon stem with light,
Fruitful and verdant garden with flower buds,
Thetyos serenity that soothes the sight of all,
Holy and choir of the pious te Deum of worshipers,
Glorious and the best ruler of all things,
Liberal and serene endowed with holiness,
He presides with equity and purity of heart,
Who trembles at the loftiness of the proud and reprobate,
Who honors the good with royal generosity of his own free will.
Peaceful and blessed he becomes like a vineyard,
an image of the Trinity worthy of the lot of the heavens.

CHAPTER X. But among these things there is another thing to be known, since, as the wise say, there are eight pillars which strongly support the kingdom of the just king. The first pillar is truth in all royal matters. The second pillar is patience in all business. Thirdly, generosity in gifts. Fourth, persuasiveness or affability in words. Fifth, the correction and destruction of evils. Sixth, the friendship and exaltation of the good. The seventh column is a light tax on the people. Eighth, equity of judgment between the rich and the poor. These, then, are the eight pillars which establish the kingdom of the righteous prince even in this world, and lead to the eternal stability of glory.

No fabric holds a stable form over time,
if it is not supported by its supports.
Nor can temples be stabilized by the splendor of light,
nor can halls and kings without their firmness.
The public affairs, propitiating God, demand that a just ruler stand
thus on the pillars of his own.
The first column shines with the beautiful beauty of truth.
But the patient government rightly holds the second.
The third gives gifts to the right hand.
And the fourth sweet words sound flattering.
Fifth represses the wicked, and shines with wonder and zeal.

The powerful sixth rejoices to magnify the good.
The seventh is merciful to the people and lightens the tribute.
Ast eighth rules the balance of justice.
The state rests on these solid pillars, supported by pillars,
just as Mount Zion remains stable on these.

CHAPTER XI. Since, therefore, the eminence of the royal power is supported by these eight pillars, it is fitting that a ruler who is dear to God should put his personal interests behind those of the ecclesiastical, so that in so far as he is mindful of the benefits of God which the divine grace has granted him, he may honor the benefactor in such benefits. But then the good prince is known to honor the Most High, when he becomes the steward, helper, and protector of those who labor in the Dominical field. For it is certain that the Almighty disposes the causes of the earthly prince with his mercy so much more propitiously, as he sees that he is concerned about his own cause, namely that of the holy Church. Therefore, a prudent ruler should strive to do what is pleasing to God, if he himself desires that God should do what is prosperous and glorious for him. And let him provide with careful care to the extent that he orders synodal assemblies to be held twice or thrice every year, so that what pertains to the true worship of God, what is known to pertain to the reverence of his churches, and to the honor of the priests, or what has been done against the commandments of the Lord, in his reverence and let it be unanimously discussed in the assembly, that whatever has been done well may be strengthened; if indeed they have been badly done, let them be corrected for the better. Where the superiors themselves ought to be investigated in what manner they perform their ministries, or how they can inform the people entrusted to them both with heavenly doctrine and imbue them with an example of holy conduct. If all these things are carefully handled with the unanimity of peace and canonical justice, the fruitful benefit of the holy Church is produced, and the reverend rector, by whose benevolent deliberation and authority these things are done, a great nursery of merit is propagated. For the most precious crown of a religious prince is the holy council of bishops, in which the most famous emperor Constantine, the most famous, exulted in the Lord and boasted in the Lord, who gathered from almost all the nations under heaven, to whom the gospel of Christ had been preached, more than three hundred bishops, most holy men, shining both with doctrine and with miracles , because of the discussion of the Catholic faith into one, that is, the Nicaean, assembled the council. Hence and heretofore the Christian custom has commanded that a synodal assembly be decided among all the orthodox heads of the Churches, for the necessary interests of the holy Church, which must be investigated only by synodal councils and determined by canonical sanctions. Wherefore a king must be cautious and humble and very circumspect; nor presume to judge anything of ecclesiastical affairs, before he knows the synodal statutes. Indeed, ecclesiastical judgments are very dangerous before God, unless they are brought forth with the greatest justice; especially if by slanderous accusers and false witnesses those who are innocent are examined in absentia, which is alien to Christianity. Hence it is also read in the Gospel: Does our law judge a man unless it first hears from him and knows what he is doing? (John 7:51.) Pius the rector, therefore, like a luminous pupil, should first pay clear attention to what is just and legitimate according to the canonical sanctions of the holy bishops; then let him apply the consent and support of authority to those things which are true and just. But by himself he should by no means be prejudiced against such, lest perhaps by going astray before the sight of the Lord he incurs some detestable fault.

Whence the venerable Emperor Valentinian of memory, when he was asked by the holy bishops to what extent he would deign to attend to the amendment of the sacred dogma, he said to me, since I am the least of the people, it is not right for me to scrutinize such things; But the priests, who have this concern, will gather among themselves where they will. And indeed, the emperor said these things, endowed both with the virtue of humility and fortified with the fear of God, lest he should perhaps offend the Most High if he preferred his own opinion to those of others. Constantine, the great and most wise emperor, did this very thing, as I have said, trusting not in his own, but in the prudence of the saints and the wisdom of the bishops. This blessed Jovinianus, a prince beloved of God, kept his faith unshakable, who, while he was an enemy of Arian perfidy and a follower of the decrees of the Council of Nicaea, procured for himself the glory of an eternal kingdom from the momentary pinnacle of an earthly empire. What shall I say about the two most sacred emperors, Theodosius, by divine grace? who in so far pleased the Almighty, that they should subdue the purple royal scepters, and also the scepters, and the pinnacle of the imperial dignity, by the inspiration of the Lord by the divine precepts

ON CHRISTIAN RULERS

and canonical institutions, and that they should always have a pious zeal towards the churches of God, and tireless charity. Wherefore the Lord of the universe exalted them on earth, and after the present glory of happiness, as his beloved ministers, he beatifies forever in the heavens. But if anyone is a rival in the glory of so many princes, if any Christian ruler desires to reign happily and gloriously in this world, and strives to reach the palm of eternal bliss, let him imitate their most faithful devotion to the worship of the Almighty, and follow the benevolent, merciful, restrained in judgments, in humility of heart meek, sympathetic in the bowels of mercy, munificent in generosity, in the zeal which is according to God, let him skillfully display lightning around the Church of God, if the association of heavenly citizens with holy and just rulers endeavors to reign perpetually.

> *The great prince whom God has exalted*
> *To preside over the people with his scepter,*
> *He must submit himself well to Celsitron.*
> *He orders the wicked kings of the earth.*
> *For this reason, let the governor provide for the honors*
> *of the most excellent superiors whom God has brought,*
> *to whom it pleases Olli who rules all things,*
> *the greatest arbiter who bestows the kingdom.*
> *He is magnified by whoever worships him,*
> *with the Word, with a pious heart, with government, with morals.*
> *Whoever favors Christ and the Church,*
> *the keeper of the canons, the leader and the best,*
> *shining with the lineage of Claret justice,*
> *is a rightly sacred King who*
> *keeps the sacred dogmas and decrees of the Fathers in all things.*
> *The pontifical choir glorifies him,*
> *As the jewels shine in his diadem,*
> *As violets and lilies decorate the field,*
> *And bright stars illuminate the pole.*

CHAPTER XII. It is necessary for a modest ruler to be endowed with the virtue of humility and obedience, so that he may recognize in himself the virtues of humility and obedience, which he loves in his subjects. Therefore, if it happens that he is criticized by the wise, he must be bitterly sorry that he is indeed reprehensible, and he hastens to run directly to the medicines of penitence; and he who had sinned willingly, let him willingly and gratefully receive the rod of correction; and before the Creator shakes his hand to strike, let him take great care in the correction of the crime he has committed, lest the judge, who is afterwards more sharply restrained, may strike, as he waits longer and more mercifully. Let the face of the Lord be troubled in confession, if any ruler of the kingdom has sinned in secret or in public. How is it read of the holy king and prophet David, who when, after the rape of Bathsheba and the murder committed against Uriah the Hittite, was rebuked by Nathan the prophet, he was not indignant at the accuser, but was already angry with himself, recognizing his sin; and he who rejoiced after the guilt committed, himself wept through bitter penitence. Hence, he who has committed grievous crimes before the Lord has earned forgiveness with tears, and from the fountain of tears he comes to a heap of joys, as he says elsewhere: Those who sow in tears reap in exultation, and the rest. (Ps. 25:5.)

But also, that which is related of the admirable humility and penitence of the glorious prince Theodosius, and it seems not to be overlooked, that when he came to Milan after the unjust slaughter of many thousands, and solemnly wished to enter the sacred temple, Saint Ambrose met him outside, hearing of such a defeat, full of great groans. to the doors, and with these words prevented him from entering the sacred threshold: Do you not know, emperor, what is the greatness of the murders committed by you? Does your mind not recognize the magnitude of the presumption behind the cause of such fury? But perhaps the power of government prevents the recognition of sin. With what eyes, then, will you look at the common temple of the Lord? With what feet will you tread on that holy floor? How can you stretch out the hands from which blood still drips unjustly? How will you receive the holy body of God with such hands? With what presumption will you take the cup of precious blood with your mouth, while by the fury of words so much blood has been unjustly shed? Therefore depart, depart, and do not strive to increase the former iniquity by a second sin. Take up the bond with which the Lord of all has now bound you. For it is the greatest medicine of health.

Obeying these words (for he was nourished by divine learning, and clearly knowing what was proper to priests and what was proper to kings), he returned to the royal palace, groaning and weeping. And when the seasons had passed for eight consecutive months, the festival of our Savior's nativity drew near. But the emperor, residing in the palace with constant lamentations, shed continuous tears incessantly. Then Rufinus, the teacher, entered, and having a singular confidence in the prince, and seeing the prince prostrated in lamentation, came to inquire the cause of the tears. But he, groaning most bitterly and shedding more vehement tears, says he, Rufinus, you play and do not feel my evils; But I lament and lament my calamity, because indeed the temples of God are open to servants and beggars, and they gladly worship their own Lord, but for me there is no entrance to him. Moreover, the heavens were also closed. Saying these things, every word broke out with sobs. Ambrose had persuaded him to reconcile the same with the blessed Rufinus, but he had not been able, the emperor knowing these things already in the middle of the street, I go on, says he, and received just insults to his face.

And when he had arrived at the sacred threshold, he did not presume to enter the holy basilica, but coming to the elder, and finding him residing in the hall, begged him to loosen his bonds. But he said that his presence was tyrannical, and that he was harassing Theodosius against God and trampling on his laws. True emperor, says he, I do not rise against ecclesiastical sanctions, nor unjustly attempt to enter the sacred thresholds, but I ask you to loosen my bonds, and to implore the Lord's common clemency for me, and not close the door to me, which our Lord has opened to all who do penance. Then the ancients said, How did you show repentance after so many iniquities? With what medicines have you treated incurable wounds and bruises? But, said the emperor, it is your duty to teach and to administer the medicines, but to receive my offerings. On hearing these words of the emperor, which showed his humility and his spontaneous penitence to undertake the affliction, St. Ambrose applied to him salutary medicine for so many wounds, for which the emperor, having perceived it, returned great thanks. Such, then, and such and such a presiding officer. and the emperor shone with valor, whose work was very admirable, his confidence, his obedience, his fervor of zeal, and his purity of faith. Moreover, he observed the rules of piety which he had learned from the great priest, even when he returned to the city of Constantinople. For when he had proceeded to the church at the time of the festival, having offered the gifts on the altar, he immediately went out. And when Nectarius, the prefect of the church, had asked why he would not stand within, the prince said: I could scarcely learn, said he, what is the difference between an emperor and a priest; for I hardly found a teacher of truth; For Ambrose is the only one I know to be worthily called a priest. Therefore, a rebuke delivered by a man of virtue is only useful!

Hence it is clear that it is proper for good and pious leaders of healthy antipathies, like spiritual physicians, to humbly and willingly listen to corrections, as Solomon testifies, who says: He who instructs the wise and the obedient ear has a golden earring and a shining pearl (Prov. 25:12). For it is better to be rebuked by a wise man than to be deceived by the flattery of fools. For if we ardently desire the healing of the wounds of our bodies by physicians, and are not ashamed to show them in the presence of physicians, and are delighted in the pain of medicine in the hope of salvation, how much more ought we to take greater care of the wounds and plagues of our souls, so long as the spiritual physician, although he uses the most ardent remedy, by which is the sure hope of our healing? For just as the doctor's scalpel is not bad because it cuts open wounds and amputates rotten flesh, so is healthy correction.

> *What a bright new light in the sky*
> *Becomes welcome to the inhabitants of the world*
> *After the clouds of the dark night*
> *Phoebe's radiant crown;*
> *How dew on the thirsty*
> *fields After the scorching heat of Cancer,*
> *After the savage cold of Boreas,*
> *the spring and flowery spring;*
> *Thus, by anticipating the*
> *soul's pleasure, it becomes a dear medicine.*
> *Sicknesses are cured of the pangs.*
> *Take careful care of the savvy*
> *maids if they spread so many*
> *medicines to the fragile flesh:*
> *Why is not the medicine better*
> *to honor the lady,*

pretending the rights of the creator
to bless the soul with the deity?
Who can take away the wounds of guilt without a doctor?
Therefore let the rulers beware;
If they languish in mind with vices;
Let physicians and experts come,
ministers of Christ's piety,
Who can learn to subdue necks,
Who can drive away diseases
With wholesome oil and wine.
And not with the heavenly herbs
created by the flower of Paradise
Extinguish the terrible poisons.
Let them call back the souls and from
the depths of the Word and the mighty rod,
Which the holy art of heaven
Bring back to the pasture of life.

CHAPTER XIII. It is not easy for men to avoid all the traps of the enemy. For as long as anyone escapes the passion of lust, he runs into avarice; when it is declined, the pit of envy is prepared; if he transgresses this, he incurs the vice of fury, and the enemy lays many other snares by which he may catch the unwary. And indeed, the body has passions that easily minister to it, so that it can kill the soul; but the mind, alert to divine consolation, destroys the arguments of his machinations. The aforesaid emperor Theodosius, who shared human nature, also shared passions, and mixing immense cruelty with righteous fury, he wrought unjust passion. It is necessary to relate this matter for the benefit of the readers: Thessalonica is a large and populous city, in which, while there had been a rebellion, some of the judges were stoned and dragged. Theodosius, indignant at this, did not restrain the weakness of his anger, but ordered the unjust swords to be drawn upon all, and the innocent to be slain together with the guilty. For seven thousand men, as is reported, were slain, not by a preceding judgment, but all were slaughtered together as in the harvest. For this reason, as we have said, the blessed Ambrose, burning with holy zeal, severely reproved the aforesaid emperor, and he detested the prince's unreasonable fury and wickedness with severe invectiveness.

Wherefore a good and prudent governor of a state is fit to prevent it, lest, while he disposes beyond measure to avenge his own injury or that of his fellows, he may fall into the unreasonable crime of rage; but he does not neglect to restrain his own anger, and to remove the spurs of his just fury with a feeling of pity, lest perhaps if he inflicts more just wrath on his subjects, he incurs the fury of leonine ferocity. Hence it is written: Do not be like a lion in your house, overthrowing your household and oppressing your subjects (Ecc. 4:35). For just as he must fight the proud, so he must spare the subjects, a just and merciful master. Hence Antoninus the emperor said that he would rather save one citizen than kill a thousand enemies. Therefore, in correcting crimes, gentleness must be mixed with severity; a temper must be made on both sides, so that the subjects are neither exasperated with too much harshness, nor rewarded with too much kindness. Nor should there be any way of correction or revenge, unless the judgment rightly precedes it. Nor should a serene ruler be disturbed by the fury of anger, like a fierce man of bitterness, if he wishes to pronounce a just judgment, since the judgments of those who are too angry are blind. For he cannot see the clear light of justice and truth, who is overshadowed by the darkness of wrath. A strong shield of patience is opposed, therefore, against the unreasonable attack of fury. For, as it is written, "Better is a patient man than a strong man, and he that rules with his mind a conqueror of cities" (Prov. 16:32). For he who overcomes violence and the fierceness of the beast contained within himself is stronger than he who destroys a lion.

But who can explain how many evils are caused by sudden fury and the vice of impatience? King Saul, unable to control his rage, slaughtered the priests of the Lord with tremendous cruelty. Solomon also, although he had been enlightened by the splendor of wisdom, yet filled with the passion of fury, commanded his brother to be put to death, putting aside the piety of tyranny. What shall I say about the reprobate Jews? who, while having zeal, but not according to knowledge, were murderers of the Son of God and his holy disciples. But Saint David, gifted with the power of patient meekness, often spared even his enemies with a feeling of piety; Sometimes, however, stimulated by the zeal of God, he crushed the enemies of the Lord to the point of death. For it is fitting that a prince beloved of God should frequently have a lightning-fast zeal against enemies and blasphemers of the Christian name. For if Nebuchadnezzar were a foreign king, lest the God of Israel should be blasphemed, the God of Israel was so fierce that he confirmed such a decree, saying: Whoever blasphemes against God, Shadrach, Meshach, and Abdenago, they themselves shall be destroyed, and their house shall be destroyed (Dan. 3:96); how much more should orthodox rulers be zealous against the enemies of the Christian faith and doctrine and religion? inasmuch as they please the Almighty, by whose grace they are ordained ministers, so much the more do they yearn to pursue the things of Christ with praiseworthy zeal. After all the hard work:

> *And the laurel trophies,*
> *the glowing robe of peace,*
> *And the royal crown of*
> *the bed glittering with jewels*
> *and gold trimmed with yellow;*
> *When the purple glitters,*
> *the beautiful order of the court,*
> *The happy ruler*
> *when the happy lot beckons,*
> *How often the hall of the mind*
> *is disturbed by the impetuous anger,*
> *And jealousy burns inside*
> *the blind fury!*
> *A bronze pot boils,*
> *not so furious with the stars,*
> *because the stern*
> *heart of the prince raged like a lioness.*
> *Unwilling to hold*
> *the mind infected with poison.*
> *Let him therefore be mingled with the mind and let him be*
> *the leader of the burning fragrance of peace*
> *, and be serene with*
> *the shining countenance of Gratus.*
> *Nor should he judge before*
> *the truth is revealed. For*
> *the heart shines like a lamp at night with the idea.*

CHAPTER XIV. But while good rulers seek to defeat the pride of tyranny in their adversaries, they must place their entire confidence, not in themselves or in the strength of their people, but in the power and grace of the Most High, because he is the only and powerful protector of all who trust in him. Whence it is said by the Psalmist: It is good to hope in the Lord, then to hope in princes (Ps. 167:9); it is good to trust in the Lord, than to trust in man (Ibid. v. 8). And elsewhere: Do not put your trust in princes or in the sons of men, in whom there is no salvation. His spirit will go out and return to his land. And the rest (Ps. 145, 3, 4). To whom Jeremiah also sings, saying: Lord, all who forsake thee shall be confounded; they will be written in the earth when they depart from you; because they have forsaken the Lord, the spring of living waters (Jer. 17:13). Cursed is the man who trusts in man, and puts his arm on flesh, and his heart departs from the Lord. And the rest (Ibid., v. 5). Therefore no one should trust in a man or presume that no one can resist him. The catfish also assumed that no one would cast a hook for him, no one would stretch the net; and if it had fallen, it would have broken everything, and yet it did not escape the furnace. But if a person excelling in singular strength does not fear individuals for this reason, it is necessary for him to beware of many. For he who cannot be conquered by one, is sometimes conquered by many. The elephant is large, and is killed; The lion is strong, the tiger is strong, and he is killed. But it is the duty of a prudent ruler to fear or to take care of the inferiors, since often the superiors are surpassed by the inferiors. How monstrous is the crocodile, and intolerable with teeth and claws! who, however, is destroyed by the beast's belly. Monoceron pierces an elephant's horn. The formidable elephant is afraid of the mouse. Leo, the king of beasts, is killed by the sting of a small scorpion. Let no one, therefore, presume to be reckless in his strength.

But that no one should trust in the strength and numbers of his men, Xerxes, king of the Persians, prepared for five years the war against Greece which his father had undertaken; It is said that Xerxes had 700,000 men-at-arms from the kingdom, and 300,000 auxiliaries, and 2,000 cavalry, and 3,000 freighters. so that it is justly remembered that the unexpected army, and the immense fleet, scarcely had enough rivers to drink, scarcely lands to enter, hardly enough seas to run. But Leonidas, the king of the Spartans, went to war with four thousand men against Xerxes's thousand armed men, and having destroyed the forces of the Persians, the victor and most famous in the war, died with a few of his men for the love of liberating the country. But Xerxes, having conducted the war unhappily in Greece, and having become contemptible to his own people, was slain in the royal siege. For worldly glory and inflexible pride is the footstool of shame. Hence it is said through Solomon: The Lord of hosts thought this to bring down the pride of all glory, and to bring to shame all the poor of the earth (Isa. 23:9).

Therefore, let not the mighty man glory in his strength, nor the rich man in his riches. For if a rocket and a small worm are stronger than a man, even though earth and ashes boast of themselves, and exalted by pride, when they are from the earth, do they despise human beings? Therefore, he who glories, let him glory in the Lord (1 Cor. 1, 31), who weakens the bow of the mighty, and girds the weak with strength; whose inventions are to make the proud fall and the humble rise; to whom all authority has been given by the Father in heaven and on earth, and all things are subject under his feet. In which, if someone has fixed the anchor of hope with confidence, he will be surrounded by mercy, as it is written, He who hopes in the Lord will be relieved (Prov. 29:25). The expectation of the righteous is joy, as the Psalmist attests, who says: But mercy surrounds those who hope in the Lord (Ps. 31:10). And again: Blessed is the man whose hope is in the name of the Lord (Ps. 39:5). For who has hoped in the Lord, and has been confounded? Who continued in his commandments, and was forsaken? Who called upon the Lord, and was despised? Because the Lord is pious and merciful (Ecc. 2:13). Whoever trusts in the arms of a mighty warrior, mistrusting himself or his people, will be likened to an unstable trembling leaf, by the hail that he has shaken, that he knows and moves. The texture of whose loincloth is stiffened with metal, like the fragile web of a spider's web. A leaden sword cuts sharp like a dagger, nor does a faithful shield protect its master. He who is pressed by the protection of the helmet or the wool of the cassava, the vulnerable spear is as strong as the staff. Such a terrible Goliath often boasted, Whom, sent with a sling, he strewed with a stone from the enemy. He was not defeated by a shield, not by terrible weapons, nor by threatening words did Allophylus profit. If a lion, if a tiger, he perishes, if a crocodile, if a giant, he fears a mouse, a bull, or an elephant; Therefore, no warrior can trust in his own strength, even though he wears bronze limbs. Rather, all hope is placed in the living Lord, who reigns from the high throne as God reigns. He who gives almighty leaders hope from above, might conquer with a strong hand.

CHAPTER XV. Hence, if at any time rumors of war are frequent, we must not trust so much in bodily arms and strength, as we must persist in constant prayers to the Lord, and we must implore help from God, in whose hands salvation, peace, and victory rest; who, if he has been invoked with pious devotion, never abandons those who invoke him, but mercifully assists them in trouble. For when the hands and voices of his chosen ones are lifted up to the Father of mercies, the ferocity of the enemy is annihilated, and sometimes sudden ignominy and the pit of death are inflicted on the enemies, but an unexpected victory is arranged for the pious. while the pious enter the way of hopeless salvation, but the wicked enter the path of unexpected death. But we confirm what we say by clear examples.

Moses the lawgiver, when he raised his hands in prayer to the Lord, conquered Israel; when he relented a little, he overcame Amalek. Thus, also King Hezekiah, fighting not with bodily weapons, but with tears, the angel of the Lord slew one hundred and eighty-five thousand of the Assyrians in one night. King Josaphat personified the praises of the Lord, and the Lord, as a praiser, overcame the enemies, so that he turned the enemy's traps into his own, or they fell from each other's wounds. But the Israelites, taking away a huge booty from the spoils of the slain, were so burdened that they could not carry everything, nor carry away the spoils for three days in comparison with the size of the booty. What shall I say about the Maccabees, who, relying on divine help, were often victorious? Whence also that most famous Judas, and the most invincible in the Lord's wars, fearing and saying to the people, how shall we few be able to fight against so great and so strong a multitude, and we are weary with fasting this day? He answered: It is easy to confine the many in the hands of the few; and there is no difference in the sight of the God of heaven to deliver in many or in a few, because the victory of war is not in the multitude of an army, but strength is from heaven. They come to us in a defiant and proud multitude, to scatter us and our wives and our children, and to spoil us; but we will fight for our souls and our laws, and the Lord himself will crush them before your face.

But you must not be afraid of them (1 Mac. 3, 17-22). Thus, breaking into the enemy, he crushed them and took the victory over his enemies.

Not only did these things happen in the Old Testament, but similar things also happened in the New Testament. Hence the histories tell us that Emperor Constantine, using the cross of Christ as his standard, overcame all his enemies. In the same way, Theodosius Augustus prostrated some tyrants and their armies by praying rather than by fighting; to whom the Lord sent storms, lightnings, and thunders to help against his adversaries, and they were driven out by heavenly vengeance, of which a certain elegant poet says thus:

> *O dearest God, the ether serves thee*
> *And the conspirators come to wind classics.*

But what is surprising if the great Lord works great things through great elements, when even in fleeting minutes he is predicted to perform amazing miracles? Ecclesiastical history relates that in the time of the emperor Constantius, the king of the Persians named Sapores, besieged the city of Nisibin, which some call Antioch Mygdonia, with many thousands, whose bishop and rector and leader was Saint James, enlightened by the rays of apostolic grace. At the same time, then, Ephraim, a wonderful man and an excellent draftsman among the Syrians, begged the most sacred James to come to the walls and, seeing the barbarians, shoot arrows of curse against them. Then the venerable man ascended the wall, and when he saw the army numbering thousands, he asked for no other curse on them than gnats and gnats, so that they might recognize the divine power through small animals. But the prayer was followed by a cloud of gnats and a gnat. And indeed, the proboscis of elephants, being hollow, filled the ears and noses of horses and other beasts at the same time. But they, not being able to bear the force of the small animals, threw their horsemen and their leaders, shaken upon their backs, and having broken the lines, fled, leaving the army, and fled with great haste. In this way the frightened emperor, perceiving the small and merciful correction made in him by God, having the providence of the souls who devoutly worshiped him, thenceforth drew back his army, perceiving confusion and not victory from that siege.

We also read that other holy men, who happened to be on an expedition with the Christian people at one time, fought against the enemy more by prayer than by secular weapons; how it is read that the holy Germanus, the bishop of Antissiodorus, who had been sent with the blessed Lupus, bishop of the city of Tricassina, into Britain to extirpate the Pelagian heresy, at a time when the necessity of war threatened the Britons against the Picts and Saxons, because the Picts and Saxons, trusting in the multitude of their army, would oppress the Britons they arranged, whom the same necessity had drawn into the camp. And when they were alarmed and judged their parts to be unequal, they sought the help of the holy ones. And so, with the apostolic leaders, Christ served in the camp. There were also the venerable days of Lent, which were rendered more religious by the presence of the priests, in so far as, by the daily preachings of the institution, the people flocked together to the grace of baptism. For the great multitude of the army sought the saving wave of the wash. For the day of Resurrection Sunday, the church is composed of woven leaves, and in the campaign of the plain it is adapted like a city. The army marches forth with wet baptism, faith is fervent in the people, and the defense of arms is despised, the help of the divinity is awaited. Then the German declares himself the leader of the battle, chooses his best troops, and looks at the valley surrounded by high mountains from the side where the enemy's approach was expected, in which place the commander himself assembles a new army. And there was already a ferocious multitude of the enemy, which, when they were watching to approach, having been laid in ambush, then suddenly a German standard-bearer admonishes them all, and preaches that they should respond to his voice with one cry; and the ax to the enemies, who trusted that they were unexpectedly present, alleluia, repeated for the third time, the priests cried. One voice of all follows, and they multiply the loud cry echoing in the air of the mountains. The enemy's train prostrated itself in terror, and upon itself not only the surrounding rocks, but also the very machinery of heaven, trembled; They fled here and there, throwing down their weapons, rejoicing that they had saved their naked bodies from the crisis. The river which they had crossed swallowed up many of them, too, who plunged in fear. The innocent army looks on for its revenge, and the victory granted becomes an idle spectator. The spoils are collected and exposed, and the religious soldier embraces the joys of the heavenly palm. The pontiffs are triumphant, having slain their enemies without blood; victory triumphs, obtained by faith, not by strength.

By these and such examples it is evidently shown that men are more protected from the danger of death by holy prayers and divine help than by secular weapons. And whence the consolation of the present life, and defense against all dangers, and victory over the enemies, is to be sought most of all, the Lord himself, instructing the former people in the old law, shows thus, saying: If ye walk in my precepts, and keep my commandments, and do them, I will give you rain in its seasons, and the earth will bring forth its fruit, and the trees will be filled with apples. He will take hold of the harvest, crush the vintage, and the vintage will seize the seed, and you will eat your bread in abundance, and you will live in your land without fear. I will give peace in your borders; you will sleep, and there will be no one to frighten you. I will take away the evil beasts, and the sword will not cross your borders. Pursue your enemies, and they shall fall before you. Five of your hundred foreigners will be pursued, and ten thousand of your hundred. Let your enemies fall before you. I will look upon you with joy, and I will make you grow, you will multiply. And I will establish my covenant with you. I will pitch my tent in your midst, and my soul will not cast you away. I will walk among you, and I will be your God, and you will be my people. I am the Lord your God. But if you will not listen to me, and do not do all my commandments, if you despise my laws and despise my judgments, so that you do not do the things that have been established by me, and bring my covenant to nothing, I will also do these things to you: I will visit you in need and with a ardor that will burn your eyes and consume your souls. You sow seeds in vain, which will be devoured by your enemies. I will set my face against you, and you will fall before your enemies, and I will submit to those who hate you. Flee with no one pursuing you. But if you do not wish to receive discipline, but walk against me, I will also walk against you; and I will strike you seven times because of your sins, and I will bring upon you the avenging sword of my covenant. And when you have taken refuge in the cities, I will send a pestilence in your midst, and deliver you into the hands of the enemy. And the rest. (Lev. 26:3-25.)

Although these things, therefore, were said by the legislator to the former people, who desired earthly goods, yet they may now be suitably adapted to the Christian people, who are consulted by their Lord in their present tribulation, and, moreover, future goods in heaven are foreseen. It therefore best suits him to keep the commandments of his Lord, and to place all his hope in him, who is able to deliver from all adversities those who hope in him, and to transfer his chosen ones to the success both here and in the future.

When the windy
storms of Euri come crashing down,
thundering from the mountains,
with cloudy hail,
the forests rush straight away, the sea is disturbed
and the action is disturbed, the wind
brings threats and stars
with the crackling of lightning;
The fear of mortals will
then strike the hearts of terror,
lest the wrath of the heavens spread
the vista of the earth.
Whoever is wise to avoid dangers
with a prudent heart,
flees, fearing all these things,
to secure a safe place.
Thus, falling in the greatest
storm of adversity,
the whole should be sought by the forces
of the Coelitonante right hand.
Blessed is he who precedes
Who then, flying with prayer,
Penetrates the arduous
machine of Pole!
This bird has golden wings
with a bright mouth.
Fasting rules the left,
generosity holds the right.
The order of heaven knows this,
Joyfully greets the newcomer,
And offers her
the throne of glory before the prince.
The votive spirit of the mind

Then seizes, the very milky
Pole revisits the climes,
And gives all graces.

CHAPTER XVI. But indeed, if something adverse happens in this world to those who rule well and keep the commandments of God, they should not immediately flee from him in sorrow and despair of his help, but act with trust and trust fully in the goodness of God. Indeed, this transitory life is just a whole temptation, in which good things sometimes do more harm than bad things; because success brings down God's chosen ones, but adversity educates them. For as the wise say, the earthly kingdom consists of five varieties of seasons. For it is the first period of labor, when it is contended through the crashes of enemies and wars. According to the truth, when the kingdom itself, with its growths, like the moon, tends to its fullness. The third time is his fullness, when he is not offended by all on every side but is ennobled in the fullness of his glory as the brightness of the full moon. It is the fourth period in which the sublime likeness of the kingdom itself begins to wane. And the fifth, which is the last, is the time of strife and contradiction, when the top of the state has fallen like the tower of Siloam, and no one wants to do anything good to establish the state itself. From this we must gather how mobile and how variable is the glory of the earthly kingdom, which never remains in the same state, but like the moon, which increases for moments in prosperity, so it also decreases in adversity. But truly, glory without mobility is not to be found in the earthly kingdom, but in the heavenly kingdom. For in the momentary power of this world, and the confused inconstancy of transitory things, as serenity is often restored from storms of adversity, so they are changed into serene storms.

If, therefore, any adversities occur, he who is a prudent governor of the state, is not at once broken by such tempestuous storms, but on the contrary is strengthened in the Lord with strong strength of mind, and gives thanks to the Almighty in adversities, who in his successful successes was grateful for the clemency of his Lord. For there is little time when we congratulate ourselves on the favors of God which happen to us. For the Gentile does this, and the Jew, and the publican, and the ethnic. It is the proper virtue of Christians, even in those things which are supposed to be adverse, to give thanks to the Creator, so that the joyful mind bursts forth at God's announcements, and we say: Naked I came from my mother's womb, naked I shall return. As it pleased the Lord, so it was done; may the name of the Lord be blessed (Job 1:21). For whenever any trouble occurs in the world, those who are good, like holy vessels, give thanks to God who deigns to punish them; But those who are proud, or lustful, or covetous, blaspheme against God and murmur, saying: O God, what evil have we done to suffer such things? But it is true that it is read in Job about the good who are afflicted: Blessed is the man who is rebuked by the Lord! Therefore, do not rebuke the reproach of the Lord, because he wounds and heals, he strikes and his hands heal (Job. 5, 17, 18). For to the mild fires with which God often comforts us, he often adds the most caustic medicine of tribulation, and like the most merciful physician, desiring to cut rotten flesh and cauterize wounds, he does not spare the cautery; he would not be pitied, that he might be pitied more.

Sometimes, however, wars and all kinds of adversity are more useful to us than peace and leisure, because peace makes the gentle and calm and the timid; Furthermore, he sharpens the mind and war, and convinces us to despise the presence as transitory. And often, by divine disposing grace, it produces the sweetest fruits of greater peace and harmony. Hence also Constantine the emperor, says, "Friendships are sweeter after the causes of enmity restored to harmony." But whosoever is a good and just ruler, who desires to either escape or triumphantly conquer spiritual and carnal enemies, and not any adversities, let him be fortified and ordered with spiritual armor, put on beside the Apostle the breastplate of justice, the helmet of hope, and also protected by the shield of faith, and shine forth with the sword of divine speech. For we read very often in many places of the Scriptures that the holy and most famous kings of the world were fortified with these and such weapons, and that they overcame their adversaries, and that they brought back large trophies from their enemies, and that they ruled illustrious kingdoms for a long time and successfully. How Saint David, that I may omit the others for the sake of brevity, endowed with spiritual weapons, because he feared and loved the true God with all his heart, had escaped many dangers, and had often smitten the enemies of the Lord with a vengeance worthy of him.

As the globe of the moon grows by light,
Led into a sphere glittering with rays,

And now diminishes with the varying motion of the Corniger's world:
Thus the kingdoms of the earth's bifurcated tenor
Glory grow in a prosperous way,
Now and the adversaries are diminished by the rising of the Court's scepter.
Why do we complain that human things are fleeting,
or smoke and rushing rivers?
Do not these elements of the world vary in recursion?
Darkness follows after a clear day,
After calm calms and breezes,
At once a fierce storm rises with dark clouds.
Thus, the sweet and peace of
Litius is followed by the sudden collapse of the torrents.
Whence the flower of the field withers in the midst of men.
But the pious prince, with
a broken heart and cheerful countenance,
gives thanks to the mighty Lord, after he feels the new losses, thus offering
Blessed offspring of the high Father,
Who creates the whole world and renews it.
Thou dost chastise with thy sweet rod,
Willing us to be safe and sound like
lambs in thy sacred flock,
O best Shepherd.
Whence the cup of myrrh-flavored liquor
Which your right hand graciously holds out to us,
Let us be saved, we will gladly drink
The gift of salvation.
And we ask for the armor of the resisting justice,
and the safe helmet of hope, with
the sword of speech burning, and the shield of faith
.

And with the sign of the cross, with the radiant horn,
show the wishes of the praying people,
to overcome all the enemies, with the pride
of ruling You.

CHAPTER XVII. He who is a good leader is adorned with many virtues, but above all clemency, meekness, and calmness of soul, never receiving a storm, but always embracing the harmony of peace that is possible, not only towards his own people, but also towards his enemies. whom a pious and magnanimous ruler must overcome by the example of patience and clemency, as the Psalmist testifies, who says: I was a peacemaker with those who hate peace (Ps. 19:7). A prudent ruler, therefore, endeavors always to enlarge, to order, and to govern his empire by means of the connection of peace; when peace is the tranquility of all things, the order and connection, and the increase of the royal power. For as discord in the greatest things slips away, so the harmony of peace even in the smallest things grows. Wherefore, when Publius Scipio asked, by what means the state of Numantia had first endured, unconquered, or had been afterwards overthrown, Tyrseus, a certain Numantinus, answered: Concord, unconquered; there was discord, destruction. For the city of Numantia for 14 years, with only 4 thousand of its people, not only supported 40 thousand Romans, but also conquered them. Concord represses dissensions, roughness to gentleness, adversity to prosperity, enmity to the tranquility of friendship, lovable among friends, impregnable by adversaries, desirable even by enemies. She is serene at home, victorious in battle; although he does not wish to be involved in wars, except when the most necessary and just cause demands it.

But there are some who exist so exalted by the success of earthly happiness and swelling pride, that they are not afraid to spurn the peace offered by their enemies, and to undertake unjust wars; and, what is more serious, they may be involved in two wars, as in the fury of the Spartans, they will not refuse a third. But often such rods of divine vengeance are justly destroyed, because they do not want to accept the gift of peace offered to them. We read how it happened to Amaziah, king of Judah, who sent messages to Joash, son of Jehoahaz, son of Jehu, king of Israel, saying: Come and let us see ourselves (4 Kings 14:8). And Joash, king of Israel, sent to Amaziah, king of Judah, saying: He sent the thistle of Lebanon to the cedar that is in Lebanon, saying, Give your daughter to my son as a wife. And the beasts passed over the forest that is in Lebanon and trodden down the thistles. You struck down upon Edom, and your heart lifted you up. Be content with glory and sit in your house. Why do you provoke evil, so that you and Judas fall with you? And Amasias was not satisfied. And Joash the king of Israel went up, and he and Amaziah the king of Judah saw themselves in Bethsames, a town of Judah; and he was struck before Israel (4 Kings 14:9-12).

I would also like to mention that in ecclesiastical history it is written about Prince Julian himself, who, holding many villages and camps, was already taking Persian cities. And when he had come to the city of Ctesiphon, he besieged the king to such an extent that he used frequent embassies, offering to give him a part of his country if he would leave the war. Julian did not want to, nor did he have pity on the supplicants, nor did he perceive in his mind, because it is indeed good to win; to overcome, too unpopular. Believing, of course, in magical arts, and presuming in false hope of victory, who, while he was on horseback and strengthening the army, hoping for a certain triumph, an arrow was suddenly brought against him, running through his arm and sinking into his side. From this wound he took the term of his life. But it is not yet known who inflicted the most righteous wound, but some say that it was inflicted by a certain invisible person, others by a shepherd of the Ishmaelites, others by a soldier exhausted by hunger and travel. But whether he was a man or an angel, it is clear that he ministered at the divine commandments. For they say that while he was wounded, he immediately filled his hand with his own blood and threw it into the air, saying: Galilean, you have won! And in that very thing he confessed his victory with blasphemy.

No one, therefore, should spurn the grace of peace with reckless pride, or be proud after the enemies are prostrated with a lofty heart, as the aforementioned Amasias and Julian did. Whence it is written: Do not rejoice over the destruction of your enemies, lest the like come upon you (Ecc. 8:8). And again: When your enemy has fallen, do not rejoice, and in his fall do not let your heart rejoice (Prov. 24:17). For God displeases anyone who exalts himself in the evils of another. Hence the blessed David had not only not rejoiced at the destruction of his enemies, but had been greatly grieved, lamenting with an emotion of charity that the mighty men of Israel had been prostrated by the Philistines, and saying: The wretched of Israel have been slain on their mountains. How did the mighty fall? Do not announce in Geth, nor announce in the gates of Ashkelon, lest the sons of the Philistines rejoice, and the daughters of the uncircumcised rejoice. And the rest (2 Kings 1, 19). By them it is clearly shown how much piety Saint David had even towards his enemies.

Oh, how the Almighty loves the peaceful!
Who beckoned to the perpetual kingdom of Solyma,
Whose angelic grace
adorns the breast with faces,
Whose simplicity is instilled in their hearts,
Like birds lacking fur.
The heavenly Father rejoices in this child,
and God chooses these as his heirs.
He who pursues peace is splendid,
And his words smell of honey like an attic.
He who refuses peace remains in darkness,
And walking blindly falls into a pit.
For the discord of the mind, the turbulent motion
of the broken counsel, gives birth to unwary leaders
often dangers,
as death soon follows violence.
But peace heals dissensions,
peace represses strife and sows joy,
peace unites peoples in a perpetual covenant,
a ruler and the best rule the kingdom in peace.
Who likes charisma with the perfume of peace
Virtue smells like
the fat mountain of the Lord's olive tree, where the abundant
milk flows to drink the nectar of Christ.

CHAPTER XVIII. Glorious princes and kings and generals, having the fear of the Most High before their eyes, did not boast of the tranquility of peace, nor of the triumphs of victory, but deputing all the grace of the Almighty, they paid worthy congratulations and sacred wishes, either for a state of peace, or for a completed victory, to the Lord who gives Salvation and glory to the kings who trust in him, who will do the will of those who care about him, and will hear their prayers, and will save them. for the Lord keeps all those who care for him, and destroys all sinners: Wisdom also attests to this very thing and says: Those

ON CHRISTIAN RULERS

who fear the Lord, trust in him, and mercy will come to you in joy (Ecc. 2:9). Whence it is said through the prophet Joel: The Lord is the hope of his people, and the strength of the children of Israel (Joel 3:16). Who, for the multitude of his mercies, and the abundance of consolations, and the generosity of the benefits with which he counsels the human race with ineffable goodness, must be admired and exalted and honored by the praises and kind devotions of the heralds; The psalmist exhorting us and saying: Let the Lord praise his mercies, and his wonders to the children of men (Ps. 16:21). And to him he adds that which is read in Deuteronomy: He is your praise and your God, who has done for you these great and terrible things which your eyes have seen (Deut. 10:21). Whence also the people of Israel, led by Moses, having passed through the Red Sea, and having been drowned by the Egyptians, sang a song of exultation to the Lord, because they felt his great benefits in themselves. But what shall I say about the famous and holy leaders and kings of the same people, who, whenever they were delivered from the hands of their enemies, or were victorious over their enemies, returned to their deliverer and protector both hymnal praises and peaceful sacrifices and other prayers acceptable to the Lord? Among them, that devout hymnist David, exulting spiritually for the blessings bestowed upon him by the Lord, said: I will sing to the Lord who gives me good things, and a psalm to the name of the most high Lord (Ps. 12:6). Hence that people are reminded by the prophet Nahum, saying: Celebrate your festivals, O Judah, and pay your vows (Nah. 1:15). But how much good the people of the Lord achieved is briefly described by the prophet Joel as follows: And you will eat what you have eaten and be satisfied, and you will praise the name of your God who has done wonderful things with you, and my people will not be put to shame forever (Joel. 2, 25). But even in the time of the New Testament, many of the most holy rulers were not oblivious to the benefits of the Most High; but the more they stood out stronger and more glorious by the bountiful divine grace of the rest, the more they repaid the honors worthy of the Almighty. what was the great and best emperor Constantine, who, decorated with remarkable piety, and by divine providence, conquered the whole of Europe and Libya; on top of these he also held the greatest part of Asia, and had devout subjects everywhere. But even among the barbarians some served voluntarily, others conquered. Triumphs were seen everywhere, and the victor was seen in all. I have partaken of the light; Guided by the truth of light, I acknowledge the sacred faith. Finally, by this, as the matter itself confirms, I see that it is a venerable religion, and offers the doctrine of the recognition of the most holy God to all. I confess that I have this worship, because having the power of this God in my aid, starting from the ends of the ocean, I obtained the whole world with a firm hope of salvation. I worship this God, whose sign my army dedicated to God bears on its shoulders, and from whom, as long as anything is asked with just speech, it is obtained. But I suddenly receive benefits from these very distinguished trophies. Therefore, I profess to honor this God with immortal memory, and I believe that he is supreme and pure in mind above all things. I will invoke him with bowed knees, who demands from all only a pure mind and an immaculate soul; He seeks acts of virtue and piety, he delights in works of meekness and clemency, he loves the meek, hates the turbulent, loves faith, punishes perfidy, and despises all power with pride, punishes the harshness of the proud, destroys those exalted to pride, but rewards the humble and patient in a worthy way. Considering all these things, I give many thanks to God, because the complete providence of every human race worshiping the divine law, restored to itself in peace decently exults.

And this indeed the most pious and Christian emperor said, giving glory to God for his immense benefits. For what ruler, distinguished under the title of Christian, and brought up from childhood to nurse at the breast of the mother of the Church, and exalted to the highest position of dignity by divine grace, will not constantly offer sacrifices of thanks to the Almighty, will not humbly and ardently obey his will, and appease his holy servants will he not contend greatly? if the impious king Nebuchadnezzar honors the God of Israel, if Alexander the Great, when he was the most pagan, went to his temple, submitted his neck to his majesty, bowed down on his knees, cried out for help from him, sacrificed victims to him, and in addition exalted the holy pontiff of the temple Jaddus with many honors. Theodosius also, the most sacred light of the imperial dignity, gave the most frequent thanks for the favors conferred upon him by God, compensating his vows to Christ with many honors, filled with the love of Christ, he greatly honored the churches established in Jerusalem as well as those placed throughout the individual cities, and when he went to Jerusalem and when he returned again.

> *If peace should come, or large trophies should be applauded,*
> *no one will boast of such careless things for himself.*
> *For God, who is all-creating, rejects the ungrateful and proud*

leaders everywhere with the mind of his heart.
They are loving and meek, giving thanks to the Lord,
whose manifold riches are gratified.
For neither riches nor kingdoms make the happy,
unless praise and honor be given to the Father on the heavenly throne.
On account of this supremely divine service, the prince
of the hymns should offer praises to God.
While peace smiles, while the swelling enemy is spread out,
While the earth is filled with abundance of goods,
While God from on high triumphs over the king and the people,
glorifying his people in a magnificent way.
The murmuring of the people is far away, when the manna overflows
with calm peace and manifold good.
Songs of joy should rather be lifted up to the stars.
The almighty spirit of the world while the climates are reporting,
While the heavenly realms are also open to earthlings.

CHAPTER XIX. For whoever is a wise and holy leader of the Christian people, always remembers the benefits of the Lord; therefore he magnifies the giver of favors with honors, and knows that he is honored, and with a pious affection for preserving and increasing the privileges and causes of the holy mother Church, which is the bride of the living God, and also has a laudable concern for the honor and reverence of the priest. For then he shows himself to be a faithful worshiper of God, while, with Christian devotion, he strives to dispose in an orderly manner whatever pertains to the honor and glory of Christ and his holy Church, with faithful speech, following all adversities, if necessary, for the defense of the people of God, as a shield against which he throws himself and his kingdom He wishes to be protected by divine protection. Nor does he cease to increase the church of God by the honors of God, who wants his empire to be increased and enlarged; and about peace and security the pious skill of the ecclesiastic deals with those who desire to obtain transitory and eternal peace and security. Let him therefore be a strong imitator of those princes who before him reigned justly and piously in the will of God, and governed the Christian people well, and fostered the Church of Christ with suitable consolation, always keeping before their eyes the fear of God and the hope of heavenly reward, and all that they did or planned according to hastening to accomplish his will, not consenting to the iniquities of the wicked, but transmuting the wicked in a direct and supreme effort according to the balance of justice. For they knew that he who can make amends and neglects it, without a doubt makes himself a partaker of the crime, as it is told in the books of the Kings of the priest of Heli, who transgressed against his sons in divine worship, and who forced the people to offer their offerings to God, moreover, with the women who were watching at the door He spared those sleeping in the tent, and did not rebuke them sharply with paternal authority. What vengeance came upon them, and upon all the people! For the children themselves, together with the ark of the Lord, and the whole people were delivered into the hands of the Philistines, and Israel was slain with a very great blow, so that thirty thousand footmen fell there, as the ark of the Lord was taken. The two sons of Heli, Ophni and Phineus, also died, and Heli himself, when he heard that the ark of God had been taken and that his sons were dead, fell backwards from his saddle and died with his neck broken. And so the priesthood was removed from his house and transferred to another house; nor did any of the descendants of Heli minister any longer in the temple of the Lord.

Accordingly, considering this example and others similar to those mentioned in the sacred Scriptures, the most sacred princes and governors did not receive the persons of flatterers, who mixed the honey of the sweetness of words with the poison of false persuasion, nor did they consent to the frauds of the wicked who carelessly flattered them; for if they consent to such wickedness, not only the sinners themselves, but also those who consent to them, will likewise perish. And good and prudent kings, since they themselves live righteously, with pious zeal rebuke and correct transgressors in a disciplined manner; whence they obtain for themselves a double reward from the Lord, while they reprove evil in their subjects, and seek to provoke them to good by word and example. For it is necessary for God to have a ruler lovable, whom the divine ordination willed to be his vicar in the government of his church and gives him power over both orders of superiors and subjects, so that he may decide for each person what is just, and under his dispensation the first order may be faithfully submitted by devout obedience. And therefore, there must be a laudable intention in a good ruler, and he must provide it with good diligence, in so far as the superiors of the churches of God hold their place legitimately, and for this support he gives them royal clemency, so that they are able to perform their duty fully according to the commandments of God and the institutions of the sacred canons. nor should the worldly powers become an impediment to them, but rather favor the preservation of the faith of God and the perfecting of the worship of justice. And therefore, as we have foretold in the foregoing, it is necessary to hold a synodal meeting every year, where ecclesiastical law and affairs are justly and legitimately discussed. Therefore, a good and pious ruler must see to it very carefully that the sanctification of the name of the Lord, which remains in the places consecrated to God without any criticism, is preserved as far as possible. And let such governors and stewards be appointed among them, who, without insatiable avarice and lust, treat divine things well, and give sufficient sustenance and clothing to God's servants and maidservants, and to widows and orphans and the poor, according to the canons, first of all, provide a worthy provision, and a service befitting an orthodox king in matters of affairs. let them present what remains; so that in the first order that which belongs to the divine should be done, and in the next that which belongs to the human. For if care is to be taken with regard to the carnal soldiers, in so far as all necessary expenses are expended on them; and those who labor more in the tumults of war, and become more devoted, stronger, and more useful to the progress of the state, receive more reward and honor; how much more should we provide for the spiritual soldiers of Christ, by whose holy labors and prayers the state itself is kept safe and unharmed? Visible and invisible enemies are also overcome, and a wealth of temporal things is accumulated with the success of the event. The holy angels are invited to help the people, the serenity of peace is restored, the government is expanded. Finally, the royal dignity and honor are long and successfully extended by power, and the sons of sons are ennobled at the summit of the kingdom.

> *Orthodox and blessed that ruler stands out,*
> *Who is filled with the fear of God and fervent with love*
> *He always puts before the*
> *Christian affairs of the court, who everywhere grows in high glory.*
> *He who preserves every privilege in a pious manner,*
> *so that the bride of Christ, the candidate of the king, may rejoice.*
> *He who keeps away the ravenous wolves with royal equity,*
> *lest the Christians be oppressed by the wicked flocks.*
> *He is zealous and insistent, burning like lightning,*

Flashing and avenging the sword in pursuit of the reprobate.
He hides the golden words with modest ears,
Let not the honey of the suggestive mouth give toxic poisons.
For the colossus wears sweet words in his mouth, and
in his heart and in his bosom, he holds back the fury devices.
A Christian arbiter resists these men.
Know the custom and order of the laws and the rules of the country,
and worship God's ministers shining with holiness,
who know how to please God with their mouth, heart, and manners.
With these blessed prayers, the blessed state
abounds in all good things, like a field with fruits.
The honor of the prince is enthroned, and the trophies ring.
Happy peace reigns everywhere, quiet joys.

CHAPTER XX. But these few of the many, passing through the divine and human histories, I presented to your excellency, my lord the king, a letter of admonition, prompted by your love for this little work, knowing that I was indebted to your highness's submission; It would be useful, considering what is scattered in divine and human discourses about certain bad kings or princes, to briefly deflorate into one essay; whence your genius may be pleased, and our devotion to your brightness of intelligence may be manifested in kind submission. Thus, the bees collect honey from different flowers for the benefit of their masters, who arrange their favorite honeycombs in an artistic arrangement.

Therefore, read these counsels as a handbook for your sagacity of genius, going over them often, so far as it can more easily perceive how much evil there is for the bad, and how much good the heavenly and divine justice repays good rulers. For he repaid the reprobates with present offenses, calamities, captivity, bereavement of children, destruction of friends, sterility of crops, intolerable pestilences, short and unhappy days, long sicknesses, worst deaths, and, moreover, eternal punishments; thus, on the contrary, he bestows on the just and holy rulers much comfort in the present, an abundance of riches, the glory of triumphs, the tranquility of peace, the excellent character of his children, many and happy years, and a perpetual kingdom in the future. For just as to the ungodly all things, whether prosperous or adverse, lead to fatal ends, so to

God's elect all adversities or events of happiness converge for good, witnessing the Apostle who says: But all things converge for good to those who are called saints according to their purpose (Rom. 8:28). In adversities indeed for the time being exercised, but in prosperity abundantly comforted by the Lord; scorned by the pride of the proud, but victorious by heavenly support. By their merits and the intercession of their holy armies, the enemies were vanquished, the princes were captured, the most fortified cities were broken like spider's webs, the seas were passable, the strong things became weak, and the things that were supposed to be weak soon became strong. The air, too, often fought against the rebels with winds, clouds, and hail; the vengeful ether thundered upon the enemies with fire and thunder; For all creatures were subject to them, since they themselves remained subject to the Creator in heart, word, and work. For those whose holy pursuit was to fear and love God at the same time, to search the sacred words, knowing that the glory of kings is to search for speech and the wisdom of God, as it is written: Get wisdom, get prudence, the beginning of wisdom; seize her and she will exalt you, you will be glorified by her when you have embraced her; He will give to your head the stages of grace, and a glorious crown will protect you (Prov. 4, 5-9).

Therefore they diligently learned these arts of the good pleasure of the Almighty, to judge justly, to be humble and benevolent towards the good, but proud and inveterate towards the bad; to feed the poor, to help the churches of God, and not to place hope in a transitory and perishable kingdom, but to place one's wish and desire in the happiness of the heavenly and ever-lasting kingdom. Whose examples and distinguished deeds, and the happy course of transitory life, moreover, the glory of eternal retribution, it behooves you always to love, to think of, and to imitate, my lord the king. For in this way the Almighty Lord will be your guardian and defender against all your adversaries, whom he will crush under your feet with his magnificent power, or subject you to the law of war or peace, and will adorn you in everything with the crown of his grace, extending your days with happiness and glory in this world, and establishing a company of just kings who pleased God in perpetual happiness. And your children will be like young olives around your table (Ps. 127:3). They will sit behind you on the throne of your kingdom. He will give them a long life in this world, namely, and happiness, if they walk in the ways of the Lord and keep his commandments; moreover, the kingdom of heaven, by the power and grace of our Savior and Lord Jesus Christ, to whom is eternal glory and power with the Father and the Holy Spirit forever and ever. Amen.

The Scriptorium Project is the work of a small group of lay people of various apostolic churches who are interested in the preservation, transmission, and translation of the works of the early and medieval church. Our efforts are to make the works of the church fathers accessible to anyone who might have an interest in Christian antiquities and the theological, philosophical, and moral writings that have become the bedrock of Western Civilization.

To-date, our releases have pulled from the Greek, Syriac, Georgian, Latin, Celtic, Ethiopian, and Coptic traditions of Christianity, and have been pulled from sundry local traditions and languages.

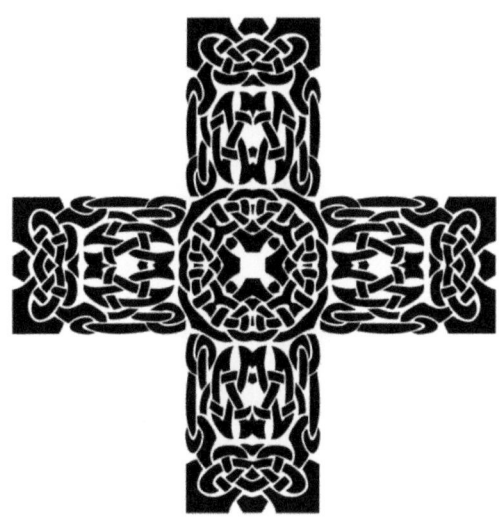

Other Works from the Ancient Celtic Church Collection (Ireland, Scotland, Wales):

Three Works by Sedulius Scotus (Nov. 2007)
On Christian Rulers by Sedulius Scotus (Jan. 2010)
A Moral Interpretation by St. Aileran the Wise (Sept. 2014)
Irish Canons by Abedoc the Hibernian (Oct. 2015)
Sermons by St. Gall of Ireland (Apr. 2016)
Instructions by St. Columba of Iona (June 2017)
Lebor Gabala Erenn by Nennius the Monk (June 2017)
The Measure to be Taxed for Penance by St. Columba of Iona (Mar 2019)
Mystical Interpretation by St. Aileran the Wise (June 2020)
The Interpretation of Morals by St. Aileran the Wise (Feb. 2021)
Testament of Some Former Things by John Scotus Eriugena (Mar 2022)
The First Synod of St. Patrick by St. Patrick of Ireland (May 2022)
Of the Three Habitations by St. Patrick of Ireland (Mar 2023)

www.ingramcontent.com/pod-product-compliance
Lightning Source LLC
LaVergne TN
LVHW052048070526
838201LV00086B/5139